This Book Belongs to:

_____

3 Stories in one

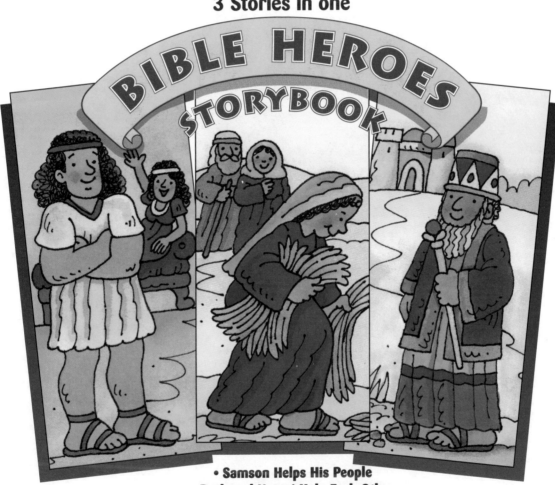

BIBLE HEROES
STORYBOOK

- Samson Helps His People
- Ruth and Naomi Help Each Other
- Wise Solomon Leads the People

RUTH and NAOMI HELP EACH OTHER

Retold by Andy Rector

Illustrated by Ben Mahan

Once in a land called Judah there was a time of very little food. Elimelech, who lived in Judah, said to his family, "Let's move to the land of Moab. We can find food in Moab." So Elimelech and his family packed up all of their possessions and traveled to Moab.

Elimelech had a wife named Naomi and they had two sons. The family worshiped God and they knew He would protect them in this journey.

Not long after settling in Moab, Elimelech died, leaving Naomi and the two sons. Over the years, Naomi watched her two sons grow into fine young men. Each son found a woman among the Moabite people and made them their wives. Naomi was proud. One son married a woman named Ruth, the other son married a woman named Orpah.

Ten years later, though, both of Naomi's son's had died. Naomi talked with Ruth and Orpah, her daughters-in-law.

"Our husbands are dead," Naomi told them. "I am going back to Judah."

Then Naomi said, "I think it would be best if you two returned to your mothers' houses and lived there until you marry again."

"We don't want to leave you!" cried the women.

"It is for the best," said Naomi.

So Orpah sadly kissed her mother-in-law good-bye.

Ruth, however, stayed with Naomi.

"I can't leave you by yourself," said Ruth. "Where you go, I will go. Where you stay, I will stay. Your people will be my people and your God my God."

So Naomi and Ruth traveled back towards Judah and settled in the town of Bethlehem.

After arriving there, Naomi saw a man working with his servant in the fields.

"That man is Boaz," Naomi said to Ruth. "He is a relative of mine. See if you can meet him. If he likes you, there's a chance he might marry you one day."

So, during the harvest time, Ruth began working with the servants in the grain fields of Boaz. She worked hard.

"Who is that woman?" Boaz asked one of his servants.

"She came back with your relative, Naomi," said the servant. "Her name is Ruth and she is from Moab."

Boaz walked up to Ruth. "Hello. Thank you for helping me. If you get thirsty there is water in jars over there."

"Thank you," said Ruth.

"Just follow the girl servants and do what they do" Boaz told her. "And don't let the men servants bother you. They can be rough sometimes."

"Thank you so much for showing me kindness," Ruth replied.

Soon Ruth and Boaz fell in love. One day he married Ruth and took care of her and Naomi. Ruth and Boaz had a son named Obed. Obed grew up and had a son named Jesse. When Jesse grew up he had seven sons, one of whom became King David. Yes, Ruth was the great grandmother of King David.

WISE SOLOMON
LEADS THE PEOPLE

Retold by Andy Rector

Illustrated by Ben Mahan

David — the David who played the harp, tended the sheep and fought Goliath — became the king of Israel. He ruled many years. When he died, his son, Solomon, became king.

One night God appeared to Solomon and spoke: "Ask for whatever you want and I will give it to you."

Solomon thought for a moment and then said, "Lord, give me wisdom and knowledge, so I can be a good king to the people of Israel."

"Since you asked for wisdom," said the Lord, "and not something selfish like a long life or untold riches, I will give you knowledge and wisdom. I will also make you richer than any king who has ever lived or ever will live."

Over the years, Solomon acquired great wealth as king. He had chariots and soldiers. He had servants and dancers and cooks. He had money and jewels that filled rooms. He lived in a beautiful palace and built many large buildings. He also built many gardens with lovely plants and trees.

Solomon arranged for the building of a temple for the Lord. Thousands of workers spent years building the walls and making pieces of furniture for the Lord's temple.

After the workers finished building the temple, the Israelites gathered around it and celebrated.

Solomon used his wisdom to write books that have lasted until this day. One of those books is called Proverbs. These proverbs can be found in the Bible.

A proverb is a short saying with a big message. Solomon wrote many proverbs about friendship: "A friend sticks closer than a brother . . . As iron sharpens iron, so one man sharpens another."

Solomon wrote about wealth and true happiness: "Better a poor man in a happy house than a rich man in a house full of arguing."

He also wrote about obeying the Lord: "The man who respects God is blessed, but the man with a hard heart toward God is in trouble."

One day two women stood before Solomon with a baby. One of them said, "This woman stole my baby because hers died! That's my baby!"

"No!" screamed the other woman. "It was your baby who died. This one is mine."

Solomon held a sword over the baby. "I will cut the

baby in half, and give one half to one woman and the other half to the other woman."

One woman said, "Please don't kill him! He is my baby." She pleaded and cried.

The other woman said, "Go ahead. Cut him in half and kill him. Then neither one of us will have him."

Solomon knew from the reaction of the women that the one who pleaded and cried was the real mother.

Everyone who saw this incident was amazed. They knew that Solomon had wisdom from God.

SAMSON HELPS
HIS PEOPLE

Retold by Andy Rector

Illustrated by Ben Mahan

One day a man appeared to Manoah, an Israelite, and his wife.

"You are going to have a son," said the man. "He will be special and will be used by the Lord. He is never to get a haircut or drink wine and he must eat special foods."

The man vanished and Manoah realized the man was an angel of God.

Soon the woman gave birth to a son and named him Samson.

"Mother," said Samson when he was a boy, "why can't I eat the foods the other boys eat?"

"God made you special," said Samson's mother.

"The other children make fun of me," Samson said, "because my hair is so long. When can I get it cut?"

"The Lord has instructed us to never cut your hair," was all his mother would say.

The Spirit of the Lord filled Samson. He grew up into a strong man. Many times he fought the Philistines — the enemies of the Israelites. One time the Philistines tricked him and the Spirit of the Lord gave Samson the strength to kill thirty of them.

"What have you done?" said Samson's fellow Israelites. "Don't you know that the Philistines are our enemies? Now they will be seeking revenge on us!"

"Tie me up and hand me over to the Philistines," said Samson. "I will make everything all right."

The Israelites tied up Samson and handed him over to the Philistines. Suddenly the ropes that bound Samson dropped to the ground. He picked up a jawbone of a donkey lying on the ground nearby. With that jawbone he fought a one-man war against the Philistines. Before Samson had finished, he had slain one thousand Philistines.

But one day Samson fell in love with a Philistine woman. Her name was Delilah and she could not be trusted. Some leaders of the Philistines met one day and said to Delilah, "See if you can find out the secret of Samson's strength."

So Delilah asked Samson, "Tell me, what is the secret of your strength?"

"If you tie me up with new ropes, I become helpless," Samson answered.

So Delilah tied him up and the Philistines tried to attack. But Samson broke out of the ropes without much effort.

"You lied!" cried Delilah. "I won't love you anymore if you don't tell me your secret."

"Then here is my secret," said Samson. "If my hair is cut, my strength will leave me."

One day Samson rested his head in Delilah's lap. "I'm going to take a nap," he said.

A Philistine man sneaked into the room and cut off Samson's hair.

Samson awoke and found that his hair was cut off and his strength was gone. The Philistines tied him up and threw him in prison.

About three thousand Philistines gathered in the temple. "Bring out Samson," they cried. They wanted to make fun of him.

Samson asked the servant leading him, "Please place me between two tall pillars in the temple."

Samson prayed to the Lord. "God forgive me for telling my secret. Please give me my strength back."

Suddenly the Spirit of the Lord filled Samson. He pushed the two pillars and the whole temple caved in, killing the Philistines inside as well as himself.